Remember Her Name!

Debbie Allen's Rise to Fame

Tami Charles

Illustrated by Meredith Lucius

Charlesbridge

In the heart
of the Third Ward
of Houston, Texas,
beneath a star-covered sky
and tree branches
lined with blackbirds,
the wind stirs its nighttime song
as Debbie begins.

A dancer's dream—
arms stretched long as moonbeams,
twirling and swirling,
she leaps across the grass.

Every movement colors
the space around her . . .

bright,

bold,

alive with dance!

But everyone knows
that in the Third Ward
in the 1950s,
there are streets
lined with
    schools,
        theaters,
            restaurants,
                stores—

windows sealed
and shut doors—

white signs
painted with black words
with a message loud and clear:

people like Debbie
are simply not welcome here.

This is life as she knows it,

down
      down
            down

in the Deep South,

where she dreams of training
at the local dance school . . .

only to be told

no,
no,
and
NO again—

always because of
the color of her skin.

But determination wins.
It runs deep in her veins,
and so she dances anyway.

Thumping,
     jumping,

                                  G
                             N
                         I
                    Y
               L
      feet F

                heart pumping!

The backyard is her stage!

Destined for fame,
hoping that one day
people *everywhere* will
        remember her name!

In the shadows,
Mama sees the promise Debbie holds
as this little dancer's dream
ignites and unfolds.

When the song ends,
Debbie takes a bow
as trees and birds fill the sky
with thunderous applause.

More than all the stars
in the Milky Way,
she wants to be a
famous dancer someday!

It is then that Mama realizes:
real dreams have wings.

The time comes
to discover
a new opportunity—
in a place with no closed doors!

So they bundle those
hopes
and wishes
and starry-eyed dreams
together.

With the wind at their backs,
they cross the border,
feet planted on new soil.

Step by step
they wander.

Curious,
perplexed,
amazed

by this new city—
alive with art,
and música,
and people
who welcome them with words
so different from those at home.

There are many firsts
in this unfamiliar place
and a few language mistakes, too.

But facing challenges
can lead to
a most beautiful destiny.

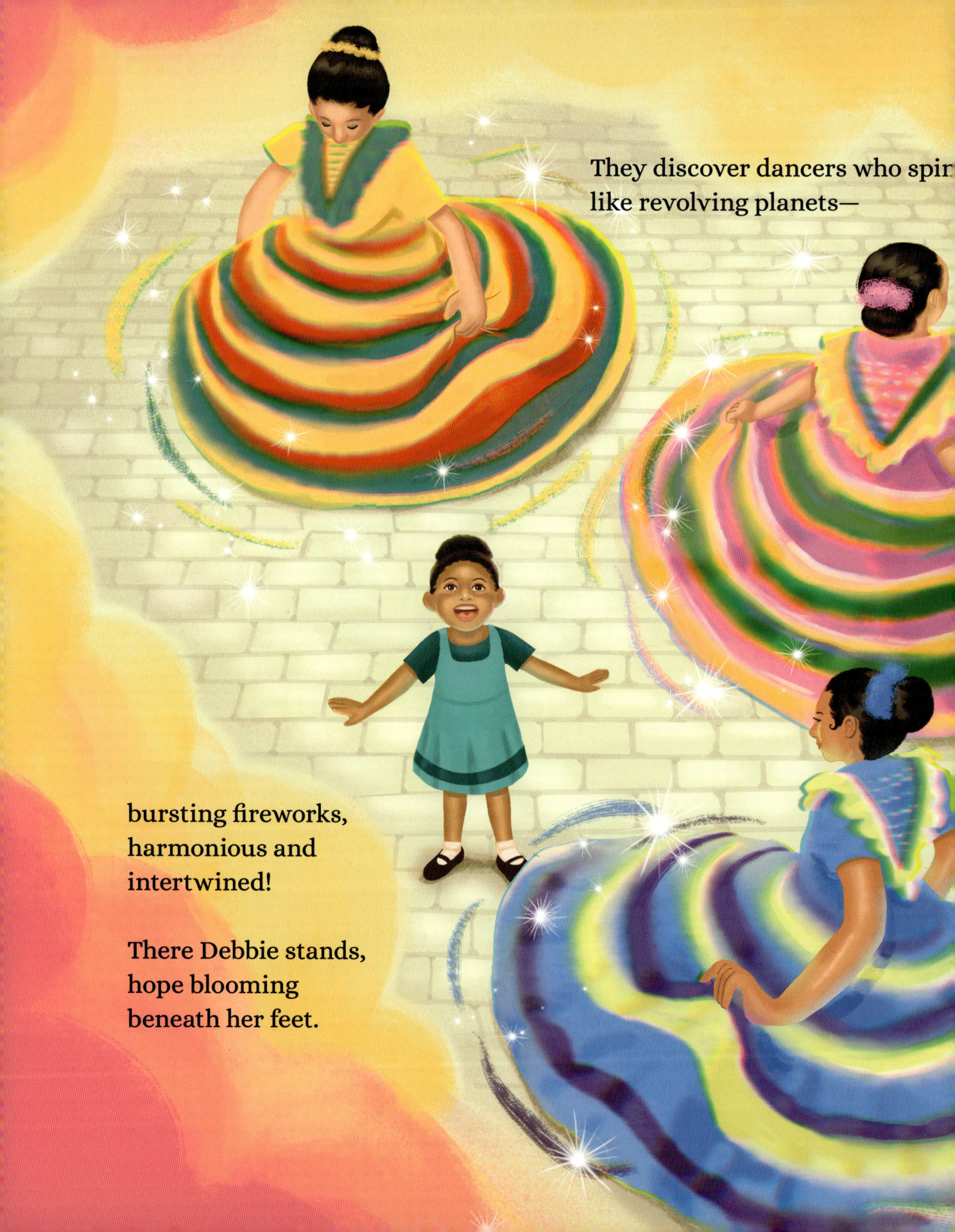

They discover dancers who spin like revolving planets—

bursting fireworks, harmonious and intertwined!

There Debbie stands, hope blooming beneath her feet.

With dazzling eyes
and dancing dreams,
she soars into a galaxy of *possible*,
a universe of yes!

From her very first tendu,
she is set free.

Free to learn,
free to dance,
free to dream!

With every class,
every grand jeté,
    she grows leaps and bounds,
dancing past
memories of segregation,
dancing away
all the times she heard no.

Some years pass.

Now the not-so-little girl
with dazzling eyes
and dancing dreams
begins to realize . . .

if this city,
alive with art,
and música,
and people
can create a galaxy of *possible*,
a universe of YES,
then why can't Houston?

It's time to explore
a way to leave a legacy
and break through closed doors.

So they pack their hopes,
wishes, and starry-eyed dreams
together
and return to the place
they once called
home.

In the heart

of the Third Ward
and other places in the United States,
some things have changed . . .

and others, not so much.

Yet still,
there Debbie is
with all she brings.

Curious,
fearless—
a mighty
brave thing.

And so continues her dancer's dream—
arms stretched long as moonbeams,

twirling
and
swirling.

Every pirouette
making space,
leaving a golden trail
for others to follow.

A gift—
a galaxy of *possible*
for the shooting stars of tomorrow.

Beneath the white-bright lights,
the music sings
as history unfolds.

Deborah Kaye Allen—

remember her name!

One fearless, majestic
sight to behold.

Author's Note

In November 2021, I had the opportunity to interview the legendary Debbie Allen. (You can watch our discussion here: www.tinyurl.com/DebbieTami.) What a dream come true! Growing up as a kid with big dreams in 1980s Newark, New Jersey, I was a huge fan of the hit television show *Fame*. Debbie choreographed and played the role of tough-as-nails dance teacher Lydia Grant. I was influenced by her talent and tenacity, so my parents signed me up for classes at my local dance school. Registering was easy. But for Ms. Allen, the same cannot be said.

Ms. Allen often speaks about her experiences growing up in the 1950s Jim Crow South in the Third Ward of Houston, Texas. Because of segregation (the separation of Black people and white people), she couldn't attend the local dance school, couldn't eat at the Woolworth's lunch counter, couldn't see a live show in the theater, and much more. These barriers, however, did not diminish her dancing dreams.

As young as four years old, Ms. Allen knew she was destined to dance. For years she auditioned for the Houston Ballet Foundation and faced rejection despite her talent. Her yard became her stage and nature her audience.

Gazing at the wide-open Texas sky, Ms. Allen often wondered where she fit in the universe. Her mother, Pulitzer Prize–nominated poet Vivian Ayers Allen, grew tired of barriers for people of color. In 1960, to expose her daughters to more opportunities, she packed their bags and brought them to Mexico City—a place where integration was the norm.

Ms. Allen fondly remembers being allowed to sit at the Woolworth's lunch counter for the first time—she ordered a hamburger. She also remembers that people made her feel special when they cried, "Ay, negrita!"—a Spanish endearment that complimented Ms. Allen's beautiful brown skin. She studied at the Ballet Nacional de México, where her dance dreams bloomed.

Ms. Allen returned to Texas, and in 1964 she auditioned again for the Houston Ballet Foundation. This time she was admitted, making history as the company's first Black dancer. This victory paved the way for her legendary career and helped other children of color who longed to study dance. Debbie Allen faced many challenges in her journey to become the dancer, actor, and filmmaker she is today. She was often rejected because of her skin color, body type, or her gender. But she continued to pursue her dreams anyway.

Perhaps more important than being an international star, Ms. Allen is a giver with a heart for service. In 2001 she opened the Debbie Allen Dance Academy, a nonprofit organization that provides students of all backgrounds a place to explore a galaxy of *possible*, a universe of YES. In 2021 she opened a middle school in conjunction with the dance academy.

This picture book is inspired by what I feel is a pivotal time of Debbie Allen's life. It is an ode to the courage it took for her to leave her country behind to explore her dreams and to return and break barriers for those who followed in her footsteps.

Some of Debbie Allen's Achievements

- Three Emmy Awards

- Five NAACP Image Awards

- One Golden Globe Award

- Two Tony Award nominations

- Four honorary doctorate degrees

- Named United States Cultural Ambassador of Dance by President George W. Bush

- Longtime artist-in-residence at the Kennedy Center and 2020 Kennedy Center honoree

- Hollywood Walk of Fame star

- Producer and director for films and shows, including *Fame*, *Scandal*, *Amistad*, *Empire*, *Cat on a Hot Tin Roof*, and *Grey's Anatomy*

- Governors Award at the 73rd Primetime Emmy Awards in 2021

Learn More

You can search Debbie Allen's name online for lots of information and interviews. Here are some favorites:

Abramson, Stephen J. "Foundation Interviews: Debbie Allen." *Emmy Magazine*, Issue 12, December 2022. www.televisionacademy.com/features/emmy-magazine/articles/foundation-interviews-debbie-allen.

OWN. "Race Issues Made Dance Legend Debbie Allen Stronger." YouTube video, 1:48. January 17, 2014. www.youtube.com/watch?app=desktop&v=f6w-jw64oQ4E.

Tamron Hall Show. "Debbie Allen Is Using the Arts to Change the Lives of Young Performers." YouTube video, 11:54. December 8, 2021. www.youtube.com/watch?app=desktop&v=hLy3SwU-mtk.

Turner Classic Movies. "A Conversation with Debbie Allen." YouTube video, 30:45. May 13, 2021. www.youtube.com/watch?app=desktop&v=7FUjClY-MASg&t=1s.

Wall Street Journal. "Debbie Allen on Why the Arts Matter." YouTube video, 6:04. April 21, 2017. www.youtube.com/watch?app=desktop&v=ckDU1W_magU.

Timeline

Debbie Allen was born right before the civil rights movement, an era of pressure from the Black community for equality in the United States. Here are key moments in her life and in civil rights history.

Debbie Allen

1953–55
At three, Debbie begins to study dance. At four, she's certain it's her career path. At five, Debbie's parents sign her up for dance classes, although opportunities for children of color are few. She also takes private lessons with a former Ballet Russes dancer.

1950
Deborah Kaye Allen is born in Houston, Texas, to Vivian Ayers Allen, a poet, and Dr. Andrew Arthur Allen, an orthodontist.

1957
Debbie's parents divorce, and Debbie and her siblings maintain a close relationship with both parents.

1959
Debbie is denied entry into the Houston Ballet Foundation.

Late 1959 / Early 1960
Nine-year-old Debbie, her sister, and her mother move to Mexico. Debbie attends the Pan-American Workshop and the Ballet Nacional de México. It is her first experience living in a country with no segregation laws.

Civil Rights Movement

1951
President Harry S. Truman signs Executive Order 10308, which bans employment race discrimination for federal contracts.

1954
The Supreme Court ends racial segregation in public schools with *Brown v. Board of Education of Topeka, Kansas*. Still, many schools remain segregated, especially in the South.

1955
Rosa Parks refuses to give up her bus seat to a white man, and the year-long Montgomery bus boycott follows.

Brown v. Board of Education of Topeka, Kansas II rules that schools in the South must desegregate "with all deliberate speed." But many Southern schools continue to disobey the law.

1957
Dr. Martin Luther King Jr., along with fifty-nine other civil rights leaders and Black pastors, meet to organize a series of nonviolent protests to protest segregation.

1960
The Civil Rights Act of 1960 is passed, ensuring that qualified Black voters can register, and confirming the right to sue if they are denied.

1963
During the March on Washington, 250,000 people hear Dr. Martin Luther King Jr. deliver his "I Have a Dream" speech.

1966

Debbie auditions for the North Carolina School of the Arts. She is not accepted and later learns that she was denied entry because her body type was labeled "unsuited" for ballet.

1980

Debbie lands the role of Anita in *West Side Story* on Broadway and earns a Tony nomination.

1964

Debbie Allen auditions again for the Houston Ballet Foundation and is admitted on a full scholarship as the company's first Black dancer.

1972

Debbie graduates from Howard University with a bachelor's degree in Greek literature, speech, and theater. Shortly after graduation, she moves to New York City to pursue a career on Broadway.

Debbie appears in her most iconic role to date: dance teacher Lydia Grant in the hit movie *Fame*. The theme song's most famous line is "Remember my name!" Debbie begins forty-plus years in television, film, and theater. She works in front of the camera and behind the scenes as choreographer, executive producer, and director.

2001

Debbie opens the Debbie Allen Dance Academy in Los Angeles, California, to provide students with what she was long denied: an opportunity to study performing arts regardless of financial status and/or racial identity.

2021

Debbie launches the Debbie Allen Middle School, a Los Angeles-based private school that blends academics and performing arts for middle-grade students.

1964

The Civil Rights Act of 1964 passes, making it illegal for employers to discriminate based on race, gender, creed, color, or origin.

1968

Dr. Martin Luther King Jr. is assassinated on the balcony at the Lorraine Motel in Memphis, Tennessee.

2008

Barack Obama, the first Black president, is elected. He is reelected in 2012 for a second term.

1965

President Lyndon B. Johnson signs the Voting Rights Act of 1965, which protects Black Americans' right to vote.

The Civil Rights Act of 1968, signed by President Lyndon B. Johnson, provides equal and fair housing opportunities to all regardless of race, religion, gender, disability, or national origin.

2015

President Obama signs the Every Student Succeeds Act, ensuring that all students will receive a well-rounded education including the arts and music.

To Mom and Dad for first believing,
and to Debbie Allen for paving the way—T. C.

To those who dream fearlessly—M. L.

Charlesbridge • 9 Galen Street, Watertown, MA 02472 • www.charlesbridge.com

Library of Congress Cataloging-in-Publication Data
Names: Charles, Tami, author. | Lucius, Meredith, illustrator.
Title: Remember her name!: Debbie Allen's rise to fame / Tami Charles;
    illustrated by Meredith Lucius.
Description: Watertown: Charlesbridge, 2025. | Audience: Ages 5–8 |
    Audience: Grades 2–3 | Summary: "A story of perseverance, creativity,
    and Black joy highlighting a pivotal time in dancer and actress Debbie Allen's life."
    —Provided by publisher.
Identifiers: LCCN 2024012188 (print) | LCCN 2024012189 (ebook) |
    ISBN 9781623545659 (hardcover) | ISBN 9781632894434 (ebook)
Subjects: LCSH: Allen, Debbie, 1950—Juvenile literature. | Dancers—United States—
    Biography—Juvenile literature. | Choreographers—United States—Biography—
    Juvenile literature. | African American actors—Biography—Juvenile literature. |
    African American women—Biography—Juvenile literature.
Classification: LCC GV1785.A615 C43 2025 (print) | LCC GV1785.A615 (ebook) |
    DDC 792.7/8092 [B]—dc23/eng/20240404
LC record available at https://lccn.loc.gov/2024012188
LC ebook record available at https://lccn.loc.gov/2024012189

Printed in China • OPIC
The authorized representative in the EU for product safety and compliance is eucomply
    OÜ Pärnu mnt 139b-14, 11317 Tallinn, Estonia, hello@eucompliancepartner.com, +33757690241
(hc) 10 9 8 7 6 5 4 3 2 1

Illustrations created digitally
Text type set in Alice
Edited by Karen Boss
Designed by Kristen Nobles
Production supervised by Jennifer Most Delaney